Fabulous Fowl

Coloring While Learning
About Poultry

FLOCK UNIVERSITY

Roosters crow at any hour of the day, not just mornings.

It took Sir John Sebright nearly 30 years before he was able to introduce his chickens to the world. In 1810, however, the Sebright chicken became a national celebrity in Britian. This adorable tiny chicken is a true bantam, which means there is no larger variety. Both the males and the females come in 2 standard colors: golden lace and silver lace and both have hen feahtering. This means that the males don't have the usual fancy feahters on the saddle and hackle that most roosters have. They only lay about 60-80 eggs a year, and are excellent flyers. It is not unusual for a Sebright to be found roosting in a tree.

Sebrights

Why did the police arrest the goose?

For fowl play.

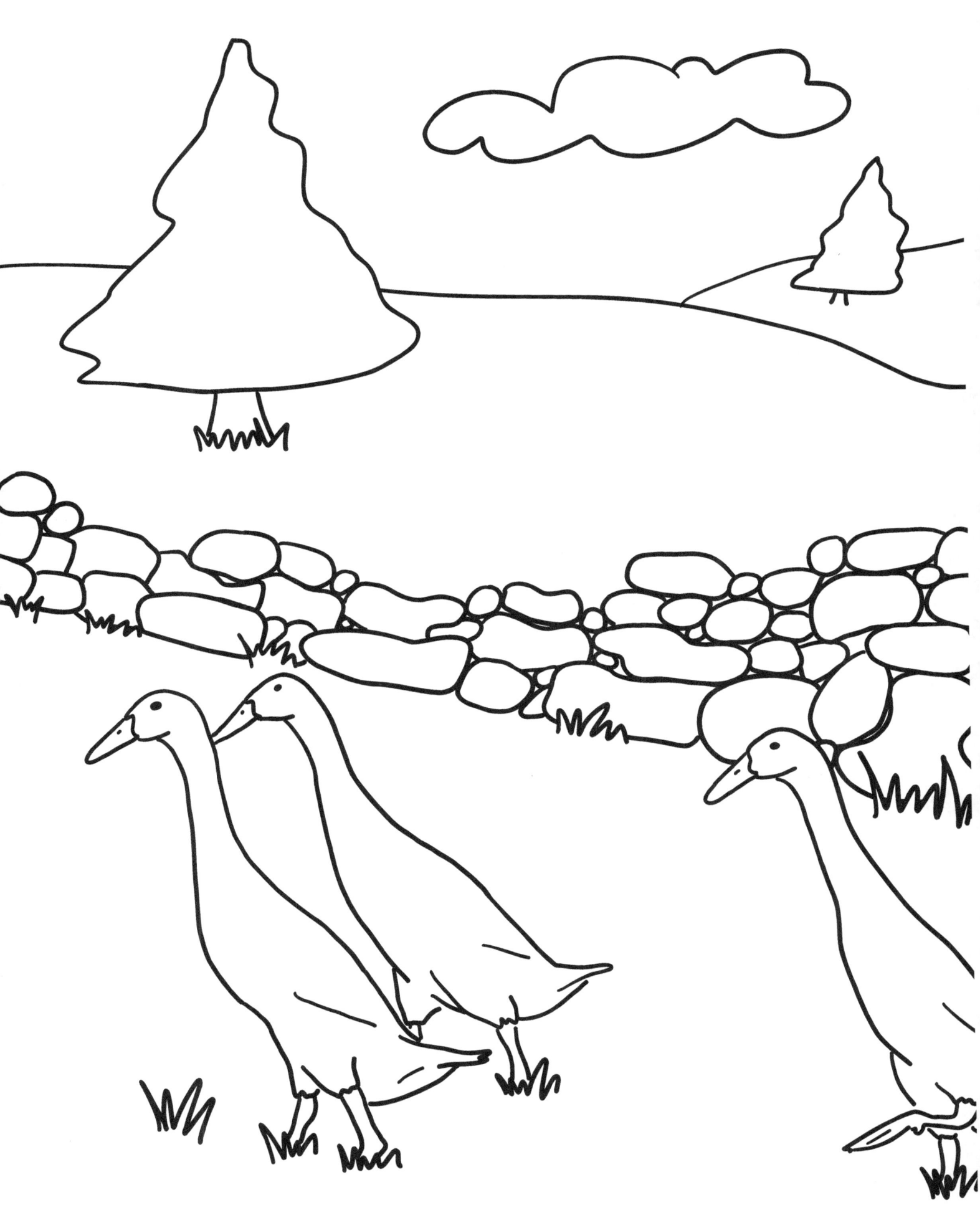

Hens sing an "egg song" when they lay.

Eastern Wilds

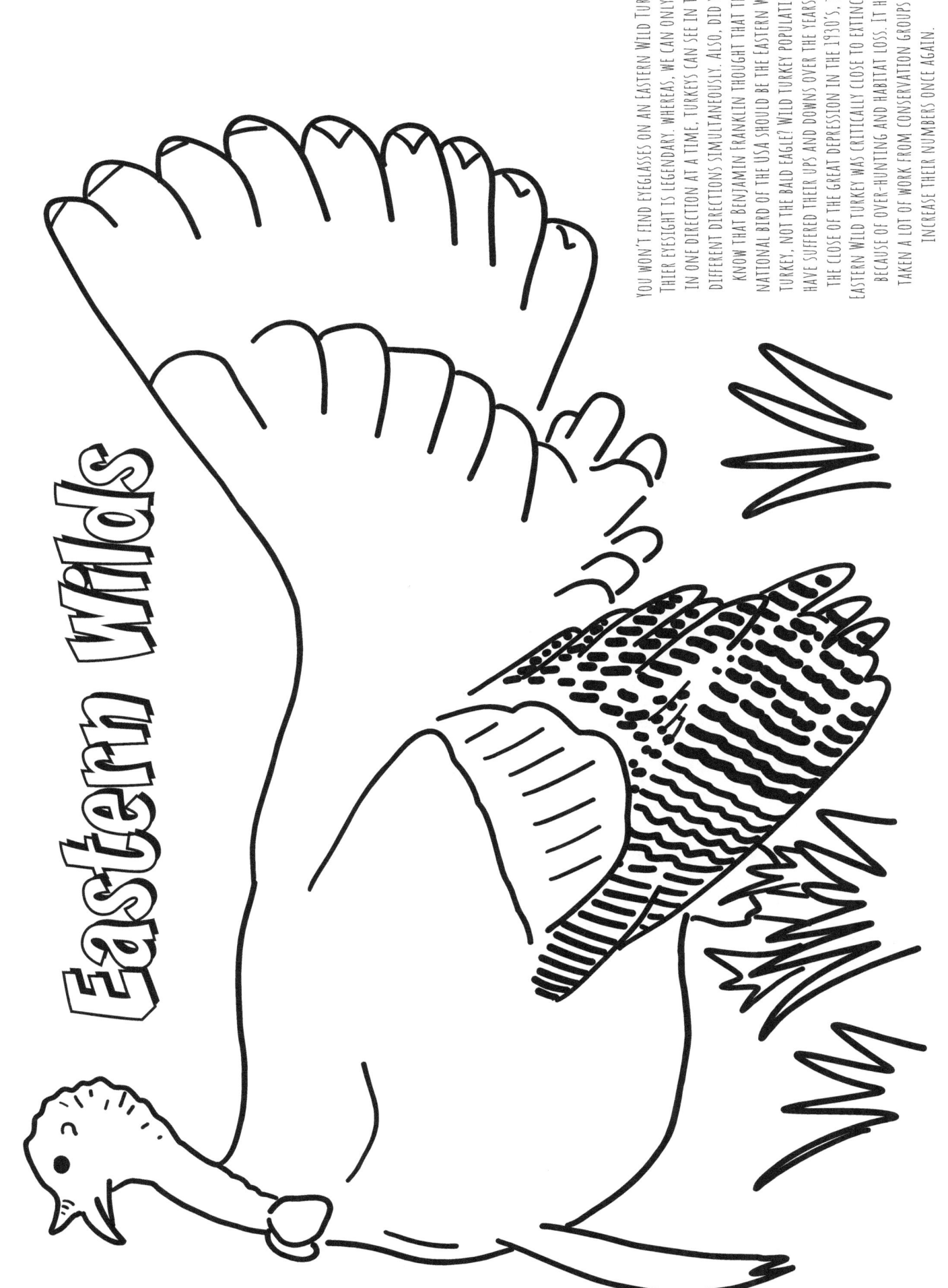

You won't find eyeglasses on an Eastern Wild Turkey! Their eyesight is legendary. Whereas, we can only see in one direction at a time, turkeys can see in two different directions simultaneously. Also, did you know that Benjamin Franklin thought that the national bird of the USA should be the Eastern Wild Turkey, not the bald eagle? Wild turkey populations have suffered their ups and downs over the years. At the close of the Great Depression in the 1930's, the Eastern Wild Turkey was critically close to extinction because of over-hunting and habitat loss. It has taken a lot of work from conservation groups to increase their numbers once again.

What is a chicken's favorite dessert?

Coop-cakes.

Chickens can remember up to 100 faces!

Buttercups

Sicilian Buttercups are a Mediterranean breed originating from Sicily, an island off the coast of Italy. As their name proudly implies, they are the only chicken in the world that has a "buttercup" or "flower" shaped comb. They are also one of the only breeds in the world that have green legs. Sicilian Buttercups do well in hot, dry Mediterranean type climates. They do not like cold or damp conditions. Free ranging is the preference of these great egg layers, and they do not enjoy being confined in small spaces at all.

How do chickens stay fit?

Egg-cersize.

Turkeys can run up to 25 MPH.

Onagadori are from Japan, and they are one of the rarest chicken breeds in the world! In fact, it is estimated that there are only about 1000 of these birds left. Their exquisitely long, non-molting tail feathers require quite a bit of extra care compared to other breeds. Besides needing very high perches to accommodate these 16-18 tails feathers, the Onagadori is a poor flyer and has difficulty escaping predators. Tail feather length varies with the average being 6ft long. The known record is 39ft in length. Known for poor egg laying (about 50 a year), they are appreciated for their beauty and friendly personality.

Onagadori

Why did the turkey cross the road?

To prove he wasn't a chicken.

Domestic geese can live up to 30 years!

Leghorns

Originally called "Italians" in the 1800's, the Leghorn eventually receiveed it's name from the port town of Livorno in Tuscany where it was thought to be shipped to North America and Great Britian. Leghorns are some of the best egg layers around, some able to lay 300-320 eggs a year! They can thrive in a variety of climates, being both heat and cold tolerant. They are also known for their big beautiful bright red combs that often flop over to one side.

How does the chicken wake up in the morning?

By setting his alarm cluck.

Chickens can see more colors than humans.

Cotton Patch

Cotton Patch geese, though not recognized as a breed by the American Poultry Association, are an American landrace that was kept in the South to assist with weeding of farms and cotton fields. This small delightful goose was known to eat the weeds in the garden while leaving the crops themselves alone and (mostly) intact. Once farmers began using pesticides to get rid of weeds, the geese were no longer needed. Because of that, they almost went extinct. Thanks to a few people who loved this friendly little goose, they gathered up as many as they find to create conservaton flocks. Their efforts have worked and today the Cotton Patch is making a comeback. you can spot these cute geese by their pink bills and feet and dazzling blue eyes.

What do you call a chicken who plays pranks?

A practical yolker.

Mother hens talk to their chicks while they are still inside the egg.

Polish

It is unclear how long ago Polish chickens first appeared on medieval European farms, but it is thought that some Dutch paintings from the 1400's contain images of what we now call Polish chickens. The name "Polish" may have come from the similarity between the chicken feahtered heads and the fluffy feathered hats of Polish soldiers during the 1800's. Regardless, these chickens remain one of the most popular breeds in the trade due to their unique appearance and charming personalities.

Why did the rooster run away?

Because he was a big chicken.

Duck bills have nerves that feel things like human fingers.

Fayoumis

The Egyptian Fayoumi is the rockstar of the chicken world! Not only is it one of the oldest landraces known, it is also one of the healthiest chickens alive today. Fayoumis were around at the same time as the ancient Egyptian pharaohs. Renowned for it's ability to resist infection, the poultry industry studies these birds in the hopes of creatng a super chicken that can be disease resistant. Fayoumis like to be free to eat and explore. They dislike being cooped up. They don't lay as many eggs as some other breeds, but a young hen may lay up to 150 eggs a year.

Why do ducks have feathers?

To cover up their butt quacks.

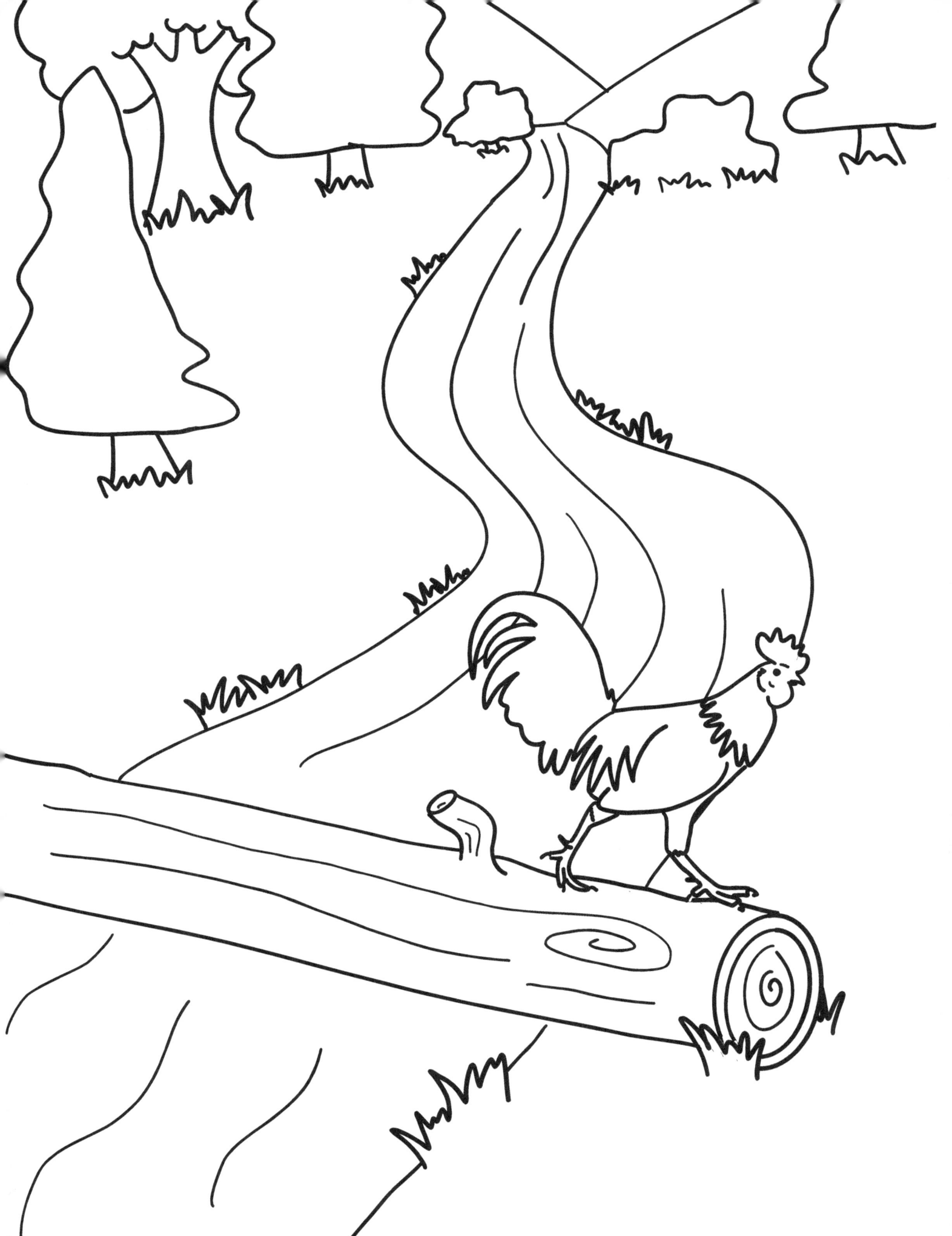

Chickens in the wild will perch in trees overnight.

Plymouth Rocks

The Plymouth Rock is an American chicken developed as a meat and egg breed (called "dual purpose") during the chicken craze of the 1800's. Until World War II, it was one of the most popular chickens seen on American farms. Once the industrialization of chicken farming started and people wanted more meat faster, the broiler chickens were used over heritage breeds. Heritage breeds grow slower (and taste better) and were not favored by the big food companies. The original Plymouth Rock was a coloration called "barred", a unique coloration of black and white stripes. Many colors exist now if you look hard enough. "Rocks", as many people call them, are very calm and friendly. They are wonderful family farm birds with hens laying about 200 eggs a year.

Why do ducks make good detectives?

They always quack the case.

Chickens are only native to Southeast Asia.

Shamo

Shamos are a Japanese game fowl that were bred for the purpose of chicken fighting - a practice that is illegal in most of the world today. These birds are tall and muscular, some males can reach almost 3ft tall and weigh 11-12lbs. They are not considered good egg layers and are generally not good pets for people with young children. Although protective of their hens, the males will fight with other males of any breed. Some people report that male chicks will even begin fighting with other males soon after hatching.

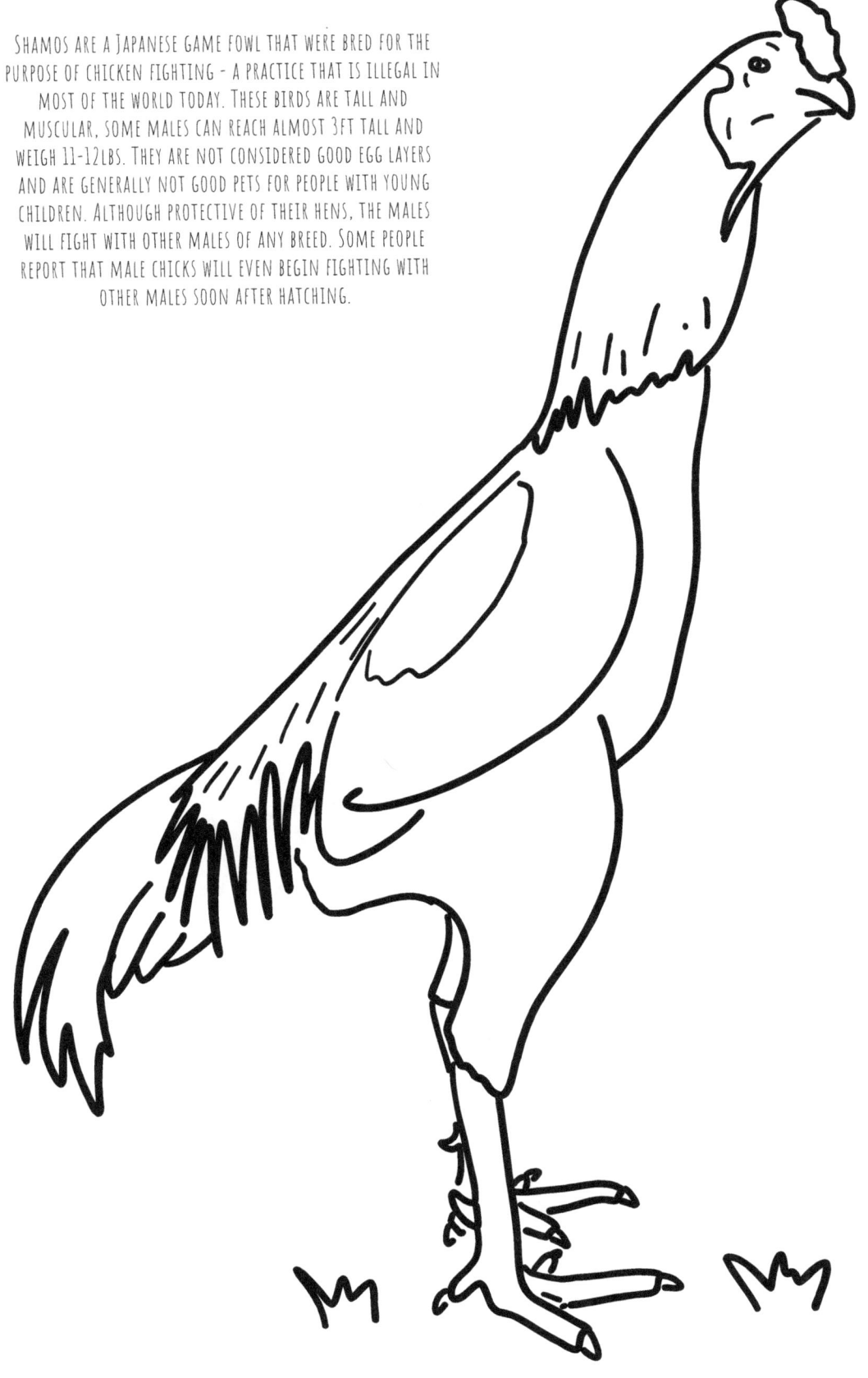

WHAT IS THE DOOR TO THE COOP CALLED?

THE HEN-TRANCE.

ALL POULTRY TALK TO OTHER MEMBERS OF THEIR FLOCK THROUGH MANY DIFFERENT SOUNDS THAT ALL HAVE SPECIFIC MEANINGS.

Call Ducks

Everyone's favorite waterfowl is the call duck! Small, cute, and sassy – the call duck has been around for centuries. Bred to be decoys, call ducks were kept by hunters to trick wild ducks into ponds and such so hunters could harvest them. Today, most people keep these little ducks as pets. They come in many colors and continue to be a favorite mainstay at poultry shows.

Why did Mozart not like chickens?

Because all they ever talk about is Bach, Bach, Bach.

Chickens sit on eggs for 21 days to keep them at the right temperature to hatch into chicks.

Cochins

The chicken that started "the fancy"! The Cochin is the chicken thought to be responsible for a phenomenon in the 1800's known as "hen fever". In 1842 Queen Victoria, who was a famous chicken enthusiast, received a gift of 7 exotic birds called "Shanghai chickens" from the French colony of Cochinchina (now Vietnam). These are the original chickens from which the Cochin chickens originated. She sent hatching eggs to friends and family, and it didn't take long for everyone in Great Britain and the US to want these chickens. It is reported that some of these hatching eggs went for thousands of dollars in today's money. Not only were these chickens huge and fluffy, they had fantastic personalities, made great mothers, and were just adorable.

What instrument does a turkey play?

Drums, becasuse it already has drumsticks.

"CHICKENS!" by Stacy Tate

Check out our K-3 educational book with workpages and coloring pages to supplement the text :)

Use the QR code above to find it on Amazon or ask for it wherever books are sold!

www.ingramcontent.com/pod-product-compliance
Lightning Source LLC
Chambersburg PA
CBHW080905120626
46555CB00008B/2962